DATA-DRIVEN MARKETI NG

transforming modern business strategies for growth and competitive advantage to deliver extraordinary results and using analytics to make informed marketing decisions

RICHARD N. WILLIAMS

TABLE OF CONTENTS

Definition of Data-Driven Marketing...2

Importance of Analytics in Marketing..2

Chapter 1 Fundamentals of Data-Driven Marketing 2

Collecting Relevant Marketing Data 2

Data Storage and Management..2

Chapter 2..2

Key Analytics Tools for Marketing...2

Google Analytics and Social Media Analytics..................................2

Customer Relationship Management (CRM) Systems........................2

Chapter 3 Leveraging Data for Customer Insights 2

Customer Segmentation and Personalization Strategies 2

Predictive Analytics in Customer Behavior 2

Chapter 4..2

Campaign Optimization through Data and A/B Testing 2

Conversion Rate Optimization 2

Tracking and Analyzing Marketing Metrics 2

Chapter 5..2

Case Studies and Successful stories on Data-Driven Marketing
Campaigns 2

Lessons Learned from Marketing Analytics Failures.........................2

Chapter 6..2

Ethical Considerations in Data-Driven Marketing 2

Privacy Concerns and Transparency and Consent 2

Chapter 7..2

Future Trends in Data-Driven Marketing..2

Artificial Intelligence and Machine Learning 2

Emerging Technologies Impacting Marketing Analytics...................2

Chapter 8 Implementing a Data-Driven Marketing Strategy 2

Steps for Successful Implementation and Overcoming Challenges ...2

CONCLUSION 2

Importance of Continuous Adaptation in Data-Driven Marketing.....2

INTRODUCTION 1

INTRODUCT ION

In the speedy domain of computerized showcasing, where each snap, view, and commitment counts, the story of change unfurls not in a far off land but rather in the clamoring heart of a contemporary promoting organization. Meet Cynthia, a carefully prepared showcasing specialist with an inclination for development and a steadfast obligation to driving outcomes. Her excursion in the realm of information driven promoting isn't simply a story; it's a demonstration of flexibility, development, and the groundbreaking force of examination.

Cynthia's professional direction took a definitive turn when she perceived the seismic change in purchaser conduct. Outfitted with an intrinsic interest, she dug into the universe of information examination, recognizing it as the compass directing her essential choices. Cynthia gave up on traditional marketing strategies and adopted the idea that data should guide every campaign and message.

Her employer, once fastened to ordinary techniques, went through a transformation under Cynthia's initiative. It was anything but a simple progress; The resistance persisted like a stout shadow. Nonetheless, unfazed, Cynthia revitalized her group, encouraging a culture of flexibility and a want for experiences. She knew that data was

2

more than just numbers; It was the pulse of customer preferences that was just waiting to be figured out.

Improving the organization's methodology, Cynthia led the execution of cutting edge investigation instruments. Client division turned into a foundation, empowering the group to tailor crusades with careful accuracy. The information driven attitude invaded each edge of the association, from inventive ideation meetings to client introductions. It wasn't just about numbers any longer; it was tied in with understanding the human stories behind the data of interest.

Campaigns became more individualized as the team began to unravel the intricacies of consumer behavior, resulting in profound audience engagement. Profit from venture failed to be an obscure measurement; it turned into a substantial result of informed navigation. Clients, at first wary, saw a flood in commitment and change rates, prompting a freshly discovered trust in Cynthia's information driven approach.

The groundbreaking excursion wasn't without challenges. The team was overwhelmed by the amount of data coming in from various sources and had to deal with it. Notwithstanding, Cynthia, unflinching, saw it as an open door as opposed to a snag. She put resources into state of the art information about the executives' frameworks, smoothing out the most common way of gathering, handling, and breaking down information. The once tumultuous ocean of data currently streamed flawlessly, engaging the group to explore with clearness.

Flexibility assumed an essential part when outside factors took steps to upset the harmony. Market variances, developing patterns, and unanticipated difficulties tried the fortitude of Cynthia's information driven approach. However, every mishap turned into an impetus for transformation. The group figured out how to quickly embrace change, utilizing continuous information to turn methodologies. Strength, it appeared, was tied in with enduring tempests as well as utilizing them to move forward.

The success story of the agency reverberated throughout the industry, attracting the attention of peers and rivals alike. Cynthia, when a defender in the shadows, arose as an idea chief in the domain of information driven showcasing. Her journey was prominently featured in industry publications, and conferences sought her insights. The organization, when eclipsed, presently remained as a reference point of development, a demonstration of the force of examination in forming promoting scenes.

Data-driven marketing had an impact far beyond the agency's walls. Clients saw an increase in their main concerns as well as a significant change by they way they saw their interest group. It was at this point not an unremarkable group yet a mosaic of people with interesting inclinations and ways of behaving. The human touch, frequently lost in the computerized domain, tracked down its direction once more into promoting methodologies, making a reverberation that rose above screens.

As Cynthia thinks about the groundbreaking excursion, she recognizes the cooperative connection between advancement, strength, and information driven bits of knowledge. It wasn't just about doing the math; it was tied in with deciphering the account concealed inside. The genuine legends were the calculations as well as the people who deciphered them, who comprehended that behind each datum point lay a human story ready to be heard.

In a scene where change is the main steady, Cynthia's story remains as a demonstration of the persevering through force of development energized by information. It's an update that in the unique universe of promoting, the people who embrace the groundbreaking capability of examination are not simply spearheads; They are architects who are determining the industry's future.

Definition of Data-Driven Marketing

Information driven promoting is an essential methodology that uses information to put forth informed choices and streamline showcasing attempts for improved results. At its center, it includes gathering, examining, and deciphering information to acquire bits of knowledge into client conduct, inclinations, and patterns. Marketing moves away from decision-making based on intuition and toward a more scientific and targeted approach with this strategy.

At the core of information driven showcasing is the huge measure of data produced by buyers' web-based exercises, exchanges, and cooperations with advanced stages. This information can envelop many sources, including site investigation, online entertainment commitment, email reactions, and client relationship with the board (CRM) frameworks. By bridling this abundance of data, advertisers can tailor their methodologies to line up with the particular necessities and interests of their main interest group.

One critical part of information driven showcasing is the utilization of examination instruments to filter through the information and concentrate significant bits of knowledge. Progressed investigation procedures, for example, AI and prescient demonstrating, empower advertisers to recognize designs, anticipate future patterns, and fragment their crowd all the more definitively. This granular comprehension of client conduct considers customized and designated showcasing efforts, improving the probability of commitment and change.

Division is a significant part of information driven showcasing. By separating the crowd into unmistakable gatherings in view of socio economics, ways of behaving, or inclinations, advertisers can make more applicable and powerful missions. This designated approach guarantees that messages resound with explicit fragments, prompting higher reaction rates and further developed profit from venture (return for capital invested).

One more crucial component of information driven advertising is the ceaseless estimation and investigation of mission execution. Marketers can evaluate the success of their initiatives, identify areas for improvement, and optimize future campaigns using key performance indicators (KPIs) and metrics. The data-driven approach is built on this iterative process of testing, analyzing, and improving, which fosters a culture of constant improvement and adaptation.

A hallmark of data-driven marketing is personalization. Marketers can tailor experiences to each customer's preferences by making use of customer data. This reaches out past straightforward good tidings with a client's name; it includes fitting substance, offers, and suggestions in view of a profound comprehension of the client's excursion and inclinations. Customized promoting fabricates more grounded associations with clients, encouraging dependability and improving the probability of rehashing business.

Information driven showcasing additionally engages organizations to carry out constant methodologies. With the capacity to get to and dissect information progressively, advertisers can answer immediately to changing patterns and shopper ways of behaving. This dexterity is especially important in the present speedy computerized scene, where opportune reactions can be the distinction between catching or losing a client's consideration.

The job of computerized reasoning (man-made intelligence) in information driven showcasing couldn't possibly be more significant. Computer based intelligence fueled apparatuses can robotize information examination, give prescient experiences, and even streamline crusade conveyance. AI calculations can distinguish designs in huge datasets that would be outside the realm of possibilities for people to observe, empowering advertisers to go with information driven choices at scale.

Information protection and moral contemplations are essential to the act of information driven promoting. As associations gather and use client information, it is urgent to comply with security guidelines and guarantee straightforwardness in information utilization. Regarding client inclinations in regards to information assortment and giving clear select in/quit components are fundamental for building trust and keeping a positive brand picture.

The advantages of information driven showcasing stretch out past individual missions to add to generally speaking business procedure. By understanding client inclinations and market patterns, associations can refine item contributions, improve client encounters, and go with informed key choices. This all encompassing methodology adjusts advertising endeavors to more extensive business goals, driving feasible development and intensity.

All in all, information driven promoting addresses a groundbreaking change in how organizations approach their showcasing endeavors. It uses the force of information and examination to illuminate navigation, customize connections, and enhance crusade execution. This approach is certainly not a static equation, however a continuous course of refinement and variation, permitting organizations to remain dexterous in the unique scene of computerized showcasing. Data-driven marketing will continue to be a cornerstone for businesses looking to maximize their marketing effectiveness and establish long-lasting connections with their audience even as technology continues to advance.

Importance of Analytics in Marketing

Examination assumes a crucial part in current promoting, furnishing organizations with significant experiences to pursue informed choices and drive effective missions. Utilizing analytics is essential for staying ahead of the curve in the constantly shifting marketing landscape, where consumer preferences and behaviors change.

One of the essential advantages of examination in advertising is the capacity to track and gauge the exhibition of different showcasing endeavors. Whether it's a virtual entertainment crusade, email promoting, or web based publicizing, investigation devices permit advertisers to evaluate the effect of their methodologies. Marketers can use this data-driven strategy to determine what is working well and what needs to be improved, fostering a culture of constant optimization.

Additionally, analytics provides a comprehensive comprehension of customer behavior. By breaking down information, for example, site visits, snaps, and associations with content, advertisers can make nitty gritty client profiles. This knowledge delves into preferences, purchasing patterns, and engagement levels in addition to demographic data. Outfitted with this information, advertisers can tailor their messages and missions to reverberate with their main interest group, improving the probability of change.

Analytics gives marketers the ability to sort through a lot of data in the age of big data to find meaningful patterns and trends. This guides in understanding current economic situations as well as predicts future patterns. For example, prescient investigation can estimate client inclinations, empowering organizations to proactively change their procedures to fulfill developing needs.

Also, examination adds to compelling financial plan designation. Because marketing budgets are limited, businesses must focus their resources where they will provide the greatest return on investment. Examination gives experiences into which channels and missions are driving the main effect, permitting advertisers to decisively assign their spending plan. This information driven approach guarantees that assets are put resources into drives that line up with business objectives and convey quantifiable outcomes.

As well as improving showcasing endeavors, investigation upgrades the estimation of profit from speculation (return on initial capital investment). Organizations can decide the viability of their showcasing efforts by breaking down key execution markers (KPIs, for example, change rates, client obtaining expenses, and lifetime esteem. This empowers advertisers to survey the genuine effect of their endeavors on the main concern and refine their systems as needs be.

Client division is another region where investigation demonstrates priceless. Marketers are able to create targeted campaigns that resonate with particular segments of the market by categorizing customers according to their behavior, preferences, and characteristics. The customer experience is enhanced by this individualized strategy, which also increases engagement and conversion rates. Investigation empowers organizations to create some distance from one-size-fits-all promoting procedures and embrace a more custom fitted and successful methodology.

Moreover, examination assumes a basic part in improving the client's venture. Marketers can identify potential roadblocks or areas for customer experience enhancement by analyzing touchpoints across various channels. This all encompassing perspective empowers organizations to smooth out the client venture, guaranteeing a consistent and fulfilling experience from attention to change.

Virtual entertainment examination, specifically, gives important experiences into crowd opinion and commitment. Checking online entertainment makes reference to, preferences, offers, and remarks permits advertisers to measure the viability of their virtual entertainment procedures. It likewise gives a potential chance to address client input speedily and adjust showcasing methodologies in view of constant reactions.

Analytics encompasses more than just historical data; it enables organizations to go with information driven forecasts and informed choices. Prescient investigation, AI, and man-made consciousness calculations dissect information to expect future patterns and client ways of behaving. This premonition is important for advertisers hoping to remain in front of the opposition and proactively change their procedures to meet advancing business sector elements.

All in all, the significance of examination in promoting couldn't possibly be more significant. From estimating effort execution and understanding client conduct to enhancing financial plans and anticipating future patterns, investigation is the key part of powerful advertising techniques. In a computerized period where information is plentiful, organizations that tackle the force of examination gain an upper hand by going with informed choices that drive significant outcomes.

Chapter 1 Fundamentals of Data-Driven Marketing

Data-driven marketing is a dynamic strategy that uses data and analytics to create marketing plans, make campaigns work better, and make better decisions overall. Understanding the fundamentals of data-driven marketing is essential for businesses aiming to remain relevant and competitive in the ever-evolving digital marketing landscape. This exhaustive aide investigates key angles, methodologies, and advantages related with information driven advertising.

Understanding Information Driven Promoting

At its center, information driven promotion includes using information to go with informed choices, customize client encounters, and accomplish improved results. To gain valuable insights into consumer behavior, preferences, and trends, this strategy relies on the collection, analysis, and interpretation of data. The underpinning of information driven promoting lies in the capacity to change over crude information into noteworthy knowledge.

Data Collection and Integration

Stable data collection methods are the foundation for effective data-driven marketing. Organizations assemble information from different sources, including site investigation, client relationship the executives (CRM) frameworks, web-based entertainment stages, and exchange chronicles. Joining this information is urgent to getting an all encompassing perspective on client corporations and ways of behaving.

By conglomerating information from divergent sources, organizations can make a bound together client profile, empowering them to comprehend the total client venture. This incorporated information fills in as the reason for designated and customized advertising drives.

Client Division

Division is a critical guideline in information driven promotion. By arranging clients in light of socio economics, ways of behaving, or inclinations, organizations can fit their advertising endeavors to explicit crowd fragments. This designated approach builds the significance of showcasing messages, prompting higher commitment and transformation rates.

Through cutting edge examination and AI calculations, organizations can distinguish examples and connections inside informational indexes, empowering more exact division. This guarantees that showcasing endeavors are customized as well as reverberated with the special attributes of every client fragment.

Personalization and Client Experience

Information driven promoting considers a serious level of personalization in showcasing correspondences. By examining client information, organizations can make custom fitted substances, offers, and proposals that line up with individual inclinations. Personalization goes past tending to clients by their most memorable name; it includes grasping their requirements and conveying applicable messages with flawless timing through the favored stations.

A customized client experience upgrades consumer loyalty as well as encourages brand unwaveringly. Buyers are bound to draw in with and stay faithful to brands that get it and take care of their singular necessities and inclinations.

Information Driven Navigation

One of the essential benefits of information driven showcasing is the capacity to settle on informed choices in light of exact proof as opposed to instinct. Marketers can quickly spot trends, evaluate the effectiveness of campaigns, and adjust their strategies by analyzing data. This iterative methodology empowers ceaseless streamlining, guaranteeing that promoting endeavors line up with changing business sector elements and customer ways of behaving.

Data-driven decision making affects the overall business strategy, not just marketing campaigns. By understanding client inclinations and market patterns, organizations can go with vital choices connected with item improvement, estimating, and dissemination.

Estimating and Examining Key Execution Markers (KPIs)

Information driven showcasing depends intensely on estimating and examining key execution pointers (KPIs) to measure the progress of missions and generally speaking advertising endeavors. KPIs might incorporate measurements, for example, transformation rates, navigate rates, client obtaining expenses, and client lifetime esteem. By checking these measurements, advertisers can survey the viability of explicit methodologies and make information driven changes in accordance with improved execution.

Advancing Advertising Channels

Information driven showcasing permits organizations to recognize the best promoting channels for arriving at their main interest group. Through information examination, advertisers can figure out which channels drive the most elevated commitment and change rates. This knowledge empowers the enhancement of promoting spending plans by redistributing assets to the most significant channels.

Advancing advertising channels is a continuous interaction that requires constant checking and variation. By remaining receptive to changing purchaser ways of behaving and arising stages, organizations can guarantee that their promoting endeavors stay viable in a powerful computerized scene.

Prescient Examination and Anticipating

High level information driven advertising goes past review examination and consolidates prescient investigation. Marketers can proactively adjust their strategies thanks to predictive models, which make use of historical data to predict trends for the future. This forward-looking methodology is especially important for expecting client ways of behaving, upgrading stock administration, and anticipating market patterns.

By predicting churn, identifying high-value prospects, and optimizing resource allocation, predictive analytics can make marketing campaigns more effective. This essential utilization of information engages organizations to remain in front of the opposition and exploit arising potential open doors.

Difficulties and Contemplations

While information driven promoting offers huge advantages, it accompanies its own arrangement of difficulties. Protection concerns, information security, and the moral utilization of client information are basic contemplations. To keep customers' trust, you need to find the right balance between personalization and respecting their privacy.

Additionally, there is a lot of data to choose from, which can be overwhelming. Organizations should put resources into hearty information, the executives' frameworks and examination apparatuses to saddle the capability of their information. Gifted experts who can decipher information and infer significant experiences are likewise critical for the progress of information driven showcasing drives.

The fundamentals of data-driven marketing center on using data to effectively comprehend, reach, and engage target audiences. From information assortment and mix to client division, personalization, and prescient examination, every part assumes a vital part in molding effective information driven showcasing procedures.

As innovation keeps on propelling, information driven promoting will advance, introducing new open doors and difficulties. Embracing a culture of information driven direction and keeping up to date with mechanical headways will be key for organizations meaning to tackle the maximum capacity of information in their promoting tries.

Collecting Relevant Marketing Data

Gathering pertinent showcasing information is a significant part of any fruitful promoting technique. In the present information driven scene, organizations depend on exact and astute data to go with informed choices, figure out buyer conduct, and upgrade their advertising endeavors. This cycle includes gathering, examining, and deciphering information from different sources to acquire significant bits of knowledge into the market, ideal interest group, and in general industry patterns.

One of the essential moves toward gathering and promoting information is characterizing clear goals. Prior to leaving on any information assortment drive, organizations should frame what explicit data they need to accomplish their promoting objectives. Having clearly defined goals ensures that the collected data is relevant and directly contributes to decision-making, whether it's comprehending customer preferences, assessing a campaign's efficacy, or identifying market trends.

When the goals are laid out, organizations can utilize various strategies to assemble information. Customary techniques incorporate reviews, meetings, and center gatherings, which give direct bits of knowledge from clients or interest groups. Studies, whether led on the web or disconnected, permit organizations to gather quantitative information for an enormous scope, while meetings and center gatherings offer subjective bits of knowledge through inside and out conversations.

In the computerized age, online examination devices assume a vital part in gathering information connected with site and web-based entertainment execution. Stages like Google Examination give significant data about site traffic, client conduct, and change rates. Virtual entertainment examination instruments offer experiences into crowd commitment, socioeconomics, and the viability of web-based entertainment crusades. Outfitting the force of these devices permits organizations to appropriately screen online exercises and designer their techniques.

Businesses can use data from third parties in addition to direct customer interactions and digital analytics. This incorporates buying industry reports, getting to statistical surveying information bases, and teaming up with information suppliers. Outsider information can give a more extensive viewpoint on market patterns, contender exercises, and industry benchmarks. Notwithstanding, it's fundamental to assess the validity and importance of such information sources to guarantee its dependability.

Monitoring competitor activities is another part of data collection. Examining contender techniques, item dispatches, and client input gives important bits of knowledge into market elements. By benchmarking against contenders, organizations can distinguish areas of progress, refine their incentives, and remain in front of industry patterns.

As information is gathered, it's vital to really sort out and oversee it. Executing strong information the board framework guarantees that data is put away safely, and partners can without much of a stretch access pertinent information when required. This incorporates classifying information, laying out information administration approaches, and consistently refreshing data sets to keep up with exactness.

The next crucial step in the process is data analysis. Organizations can utilize different logical methods to get significant experiences from the gathered information. Illustrative examination helps in summing up and deciphering verifiable information, giving a preview of past execution. Machine learning and statistical algorithms are used in predictive analytics to predict future outcomes and trends. Prescriptive analytics goes one step further by recommending actions based on data analysis's insights.

In the domain of promoting, division is a typical work on during information examination. Organizations section their main interest group in view of socio economics, conduct, and other pertinent models. They are able to adapt their marketing strategies to specific customer groups as a result, making campaigns more successful and increasing overall customer engagement.

Ceaseless observing and cycle are fundamental in the unique field of promoting. Customer inclinations, market patterns, and contender systems develop over the long run. Routinely refreshing and refining information assortment techniques guarantees that organizations keep up to date with changes on the lookout and adjust their systems likewise. This iterative approach aids in maintaining a competitive edge and enables quick decision-making.

Moral contemplations are vital in the assortment and utilization of advertising information. Businesses need to be open about how they collect data and get people's permission in light of growing privacy concerns. Complying with information insurance guidelines and industry norms isn't just a legitimate prerequisite yet in addition significant for keeping up with entrust with clients.

All in all, gathering pertinent showcasing information is a complex cycle that includes characterizing clear goals, utilizing different information assortment strategies, utilizing both conventional and computerized sources, and dissecting the information to remove significant bits of knowledge. A progressing and iterative interaction expects flexibility to changing business sector elements and moral contemplations to guarantee the capable utilization of customer data. By focusing on the assortment of precise and wise information, organizations can pursue informed choices, upgrade their promoting systems, and eventually make more prominent progress in the serious business scene.

Data Storage and Management

Information capacity and the executives assume urgent parts in the domain of information driven advertising, filling in as the spine for the essential usage of data to upgrade business execution. In the contemporary scene, where information is frequently alluded to as the "new oil," associations influence cutting edge innovations to store, coordinate, and break down immense measures of data to acquire important bits of knowledge into customer conduct and inclinations.

Information Capacity in Information Driven Showcasing:

1. Infrastructure for storage:

The underpinning of information driven advertising lies in a powerful capacity framework. Associations utilize different capacity arrangements, going from customary social data sets to current cloud-based capacity frameworks. Structured data storage is still offered by traditional databases like MySQL and Oracle. Notwithstanding, the coming of large information has incited the reception of disseminated stockpiling arrangements like Hadoop Appropriated Document Framework (HDFS) and cloud-based administrations like Amazon S3, Google Distributed storage, and Microsoft Purplish blue Mass Stockpiling.

2. Scalability:
Versatility is a significant figure information capacity for the purpose of showcasing. The storage infrastructure must seamlessly expand to accommodate the expanding datasets as businesses expand and data volumes rise. Cloud-based capacity arrangements succeed in adaptability, permitting advertisers to scale their capacity needs on-request without the requirement for huge forthright interests in equipment.

3. Information Lakes:
The idea of information lakes has acquired conspicuousness as of late. These are huge vaults that store crude, unstructured information at scale. Marketers make use of data lakes to consolidate various datasets and provide a comprehensive view of how customers interact with various touchpoints. Utilizing apparatuses like Apache Flash or Hadoop for information handling, advertisers can separate significant experiences from these information lakes.

Information The board in Information Driven Advertising:
1. Information Quality:

23

The progress of information driven showcasing depends on the nature of the information being used. Low quality information can prompt incorrect examinations and imperfect independent direction. Utilizing methods like deduplication, validation, and standardization, businesses implement data cleansing processes to guarantee the quality of their data. To maintain a high level of data quality over time, regular audits and monitoring mechanisms are essential.

2. Information Reconciliation:

In a run of the mill promoting situation, information is obtained from different channels, including client communications, virtual entertainment, and online exchanges. Powerful information the executives include incorporating these different datasets to make a bound together perspective on client conduct. Incorporation instruments and stages work with the consistent progression of information between various frameworks, guaranteeing a firm and far reaching comprehension of the client venture.

3. Information Security and Consistency:

As the volume of client information keeps on developing, guaranteeing its security becomes vital. Data breaches can have serious repercussions, reducing customer confidence and harming a company's reputation. Vigorous information the executives rehearse include carrying out encryption, access controls, and normal security reviews. Additionally, in order to avoid legal repercussions and fines, it is essential to comply with data protection regulations like the CCPA and GDPR.

4. Governance of Data:

Information administration is a system that guarantees information is overseen capably and morally all through its lifecycle. This incorporates characterizing information proprietorship, laying out strategies for information use, and authorizing consistency with guidelines. Marketers can use data governance frameworks to make well-informed decisions while safeguarding the confidentiality and integrity of customer data.

The Crossing point of Information Stockpiling and The executives:

1. Ongoing Investigation:

The combination of effective information stockpiling and the executives works with constant examination in information driven promoting. Marketers can quickly gain insight into customer behavior by utilizing the power of analytics tools when data is stored in easily accessible formats and seamlessly integrated. This capacity is significant for making customized advertising efforts and answering speedily to changing business sector elements.

2. AI and simulated intelligence:

The collaboration between information capacity and the board is especially obvious in the reconciliation of AI and computerized reasoning (simulated intelligence) into promoting procedures. High level calculations require immense datasets for preparing and refinement. Compelling capacity arrangements empower the capacity of these datasets, while strong information the board guarantees their precision and pertinence. This cooperative energy engages advertisers to use prescient examination and proposal motors for more designated and customized promoting endeavors.

Difficulties and Future Patterns:

1. Information Protection Concerns:

As information driven promoting propels, worries about security and information insurance keep on developing. Finding some kind of harmony between utilizing client information for the purpose of showcasing and regarding protection privileges is a continuous test. Future patterns will probably see expanded accentuation on straightforward information practices and innovations that empower customized showcasing without compromising protection.

2. Edge Registering:

New storage and processing options for data have emerged as a result of the rise of edge computing. By decentralizing figuring power and putting away information nearer to the source, edge processing decreases dormancy and empowers quicker independent direction. This could result in more immediate and customized interactions with customers in the context of data-driven marketing.

3. Blockchain in Information The board:

Blockchain innovation holds guarantee for improving information the executives promote. Its decentralized and alter safe nature can guarantee the respectability of information, giving a straightforward and secure climate for overseeing client data. Consolidating blockchain into information the executives' practices might turn out to be more pervasive as associations look for creative answers to address information security concerns.

Taking everything into account, the cooperative connection between information capacity and the executives shapes the bedrock of effective information driven advertising methodologies. As innovation develops, associations should persistently adjust their capacity framework and information the board practices to outfit the maximum capacity of the steadily growing ocean of information. The seamless integration of advanced storage solutions, efficient data management practices, and the ethical use of customer information to drive meaningful and personalized interactions are the future of data-driven marketing.

Chapter 2
Key Analytics Tools for Marketing

Utilizing analytics tools has become essential for businesses looking to maximize their marketing efforts and make informed decisions in the ever-evolving digital marketing landscape. These instruments give significant bits of knowledge into customer conduct, crusade execution, and generally speaking promoting return for money invested. Here, we dig into some key examination devices that assume an essential part in molding effective showcasing techniques.

Google Examination:

Without a doubt one of the most generally utilized examination instruments, Google Investigation offers an extensive set-up of elements for following and dissecting site traffic. From checking client commitment to recognizing traffic sources and client socioeconomics, this instrument engages advertisers with an abundance of information. Businesses can use conversion tracking, goal setting, and e-commerce tracking to improve the user experience and increase conversion rates on their websites.

HubSpot:

HubSpot goes past fundamental investigation, giving an incorporated stage that incorporates client relationship with the executives (CRM), showcasing mechanization, and deals apparatuses. The examination dashboard permits advertisers to follow site execution, virtual entertainment commitment, and email crusade adequacy. A comprehensive view of the customer journey can be created by linking these metrics to specific leads in the CRM, facilitating personalized and targeted marketing efforts.

Adobe Examination:

Adobe Examination takes special care of ventures with cutting edge investigation needs. It offers constant examination, profound division abilities, and prescient investigation for determining patterns. Advertisers can quantify and investigate the effect of showcasing efforts across different channels and gadgets. The platform's robust data visualization tools make it easier to understand and make decisions based on data.

Insane Egg:

Insane Egg centers around visual examination, utilizing instruments like heatmaps, scrollmaps, and client accounts. Heatmaps uncover where clients snap and how far they look on a website page, giving bits of knowledge into client conduct. This visual information is instrumental in enhancing web architecture and design for further developed client commitment and transformation rates.

SEMrush:

SEMrush is a go-to device for serious investigation and catchphrase research. Advertisers can acquire significant experiences into contenders' systems, recognize high-performing catchphrases, and track web search tool rankings. Marketers can use the tool's backlink analysis and site audit features to boost their SEO efforts.

Socialbee:

Online entertainment examinations are essential for grasping crowd commitment and streamlining content procedure. Socialbee gives investigation to significant online entertainment stages, assisting advertisers with estimating the exhibition of their web-based entertainment crusades. It additionally offers highlights for booking posts, overseeing content, and crowd focusing on.

Mailchimp:

Mailchimp excels at providing email campaigns with analytics, and email marketing continues to be a powerful channel. Advertisers can follow open rates, navigate rates, and other pertinent measurements. Features for A/B testing enable email content and design optimization, ensuring maximum effectiveness in reaching the intended audience.

BuzzSumo:

Content promoting depends on making connections with and shareable substance. BuzzSumo assists advertisers with recognizing moving themes and well known content in their industry. By breaking down satisfied execution and virtual entertainment shares, advertisers can tailor their substance procedure to resound with their interest group.

Hotjar:

Hotjar provides a comprehensive view of user behavior by combining various analytics tools, such as heatmaps, session recordings, and surveys. Marketers can see how visitors use their website and see where they can improve. The features of the tool for feedback and surveys provide users with direct feedback, facilitating ongoing improvement.

Kissmetrics:

Zeroed in on client commitment and maintenance, Kissmetrics offers examination to follow individual client ventures. Marketers can learn about how users behave at different touchpoints, which makes it easier to create personalized marketing campaigns. The stage's channel examination helps with distinguishing and tending to expected bottlenecks in the transformation cycle.

All in all, the stockpile of examination devices accessible to advertisers today assumes an essential part in exploring the intricacies of the computerized scene. From understanding site traffic and client conduct to enhancing web-based entertainment and email crusades, these apparatuses engage advertisers to settle on information driven choices. The key falsehoods in embracing these devices as well as in coordinating their experiences to shape a strong system that lines up with business goals. As the advanced promoting scene keeps on developing, keeping up to date with arising investigation apparatuses and tackling their abilities will be fundamental for supported achievement.

Google Analytics and Social Media Analytics

Google Examination and Web-based Entertainment Investigation are integral assets that give important experiences into online client conduct and the presentation of advanced showcasing endeavors. Both assume pivotal parts in assisting organizations with figuring out their crowd, refine their techniques, and improve their web-based presence.

Google Investigation:

1. Prologue to research Examination:

Google Examination is an administration for web investigation offered by Google that monitors and reports website traffic. It gives an exhaustive perspective on client connections with a site, empowering organizations to pursue informed choices in light of information driven experiences.

2. Key Highlights of Google Examination:

Traffic Flows: Google Examination permits clients to recognize the wellsprings of site traffic, like direct visits, natural pursuit, references, and online entertainment. This data assists organizations with understanding which channels are driving the most guests.

Client Conduct: The platform monitors user behavior, including the pages visited, time spent on the site, and the actions taken This information supports streamlining site content and design to improve the client experience.

Change Following: One of the basic elements is transformation following, which assists organizations with estimating the progress of explicit objectives, like finishing a buy, finishing up a structure, or pursuing a bulletin.

Crowd Socioeconomics: Google Investigation gives experiences into the socioeconomics of site guests, including age, orientation, area, and gadget utilized. This data is significant for fitting substance to the interest group.

3. Execution of Google Investigation:

To use Google Examination actually, organizations need to coordinate the following code into their site. This code gathers information and sends it to the

Google Examination account, where it is handled and introduced in an easy to use dashboard. Putting forth objectives and occasions permits organizations to follow explicit activities and measure achievement.

4. Advantages of Google Examination:

Information Driven Independent direction: Businesses can make informed decisions to enhance their online presence with detailed user behavior data. From refining advertising methodologies to upgrading site execution, Google Examination gives the bits of knowledge expected to progress.

return for capital invested Estimation: Google Examination assists organizations with estimating the profit from venture (return on initial capital investment) of their showcasing efforts. By following transformations and ascribing them to explicit channels, organizations can distribute assets actually.

Customization: Businesses can customize the platform by setting up custom dimensions, creating custom reports, and tracking specific metrics that are relevant to their goals.

Web-based Entertainment Examination:

1. Outline of Web-based Entertainment Investigation:

Online Entertainment Examination includes the assortment, investigation, and understanding of information from web-based entertainment stages. It furnishes organizations with a more profound comprehension of their online entertainment execution, crowd commitment, and the viability of their web-based entertainment techniques.

2. Key Measurements in Web-based Entertainment Examination:

Engagement: Measurements like preferences, remarks, offers, and snaps measure crowd commitment. High commitment shows major areas of strength for a between the crowd and the substance.

Reach and Impressions: Understanding the number of individuals that see a post (impressions) and how far it spreads (reach) assists organizations with measuring the viability of their substance in contacting a more extensive crowd.

Supporter Development: Following the development in the quantity of supporters over the long haul gives bits of knowledge into the ubiquity and allure of a brand via web-based entertainment.

Active clicking factor (CTR): CTR estimates the level of individuals who click on a connection contrasted with the complete number of individuals who view a post. It's vital for evaluating the adequacy of source of inspiration components.

3. Web-based Entertainment Tuning in:

Web-based entertainment examination includes following measurements as well as paying attention to online discussions. By observing notices, remarks, and opinion, organizations can comprehend how their image is seen and distinguish open doors for development.

4. Connectivity to Google Analytics:

Consolidating Virtual Entertainment Investigation with Google Examination gives an all encompassing perspective on internet based execution. Organizations can perceive how virtual entertainment channels add to site traffic, changes, and generally speaking web-based achievement.

5. What Social Media Analytics Can Do for You:

Creation of Specific Content: Businesses can learn more about their audience's favorite content by analyzing social media data. This knowledge empowers them to make more design decisions and connect with content.

Cutthroat Investigation: By adapting strategies based on the competitive landscape, Social Media Analytics enables businesses to monitor competitors, identify industry trends, and remain ahead of the curve.

Crusade Improvement: Businesses can determine which social media campaigns perform well and which ones don't. For maximizing ROI and optimizing future campaigns, this information is useful.

Google Examination and Online Entertainment Examination are vital devices for organizations planning to flourish in the computerized scene. While Social Media Analytics focuses on comprehending and optimizing social media engagement, Google Analytics provides a comprehensive view of website performance and user behavior. Incorporating these two investigation approaches offers a total image of online achievement, engaging organizations to pursue information driven choices, refine methodologies, and interface all the more really with their ideal interest group. Whether it's refining site content, streamlining virtual entertainment missions, or estimating return for money invested, these investigation devices are fundamental for exploring the intricacies of the advanced world.

Customer Relationship Management (CRM) Systems

Client Relationship The board (CRM) frameworks assume an essential part in the domain of information driven promoting, filling in as the key part that associates organizations with their clients in a more customized and effective way. In the steadily developing scene of advertising, where information is the money that fills procedures, CRM frameworks have become irreplaceable apparatuses for organizations hoping to fashion more grounded associations with their customer base.

At its center, CRM includes overseeing and investigating client cooperations all through the whole lifecycle. In an information driven showcasing approach, CRM frameworks become the spine, conglomerating and coordinating immense measures of client information to give noteworthy bits of knowledge. This information driven approach empowers advertisers to grasp their crowd on a granular level, considering designated and customized showcasing endeavors.

One of the vital benefits of CRM frameworks in information driven advertising is the capacity to concentrate client information. These frameworks combine data from different touchpoints, like site collaborations, online entertainment commitment, and buy history, into a brought together data set. This concentrated storehouse of client data fills in as a gold mine for advertisers, giving an extensive perspective on every client's inclinations, ways of behaving, and history with the brand.

With regards to information driven showcasing, CRM frameworks go about as an impetus for division and focusing on. Marketers can create highly segmented and targeted campaigns by making use of the data stored in the CRM. This accuracy guarantees that advertising messages reverberate with explicit client sections, prompting expanded commitment and change rates. Using CRM data, a clothing retailer could, for instance, tailor promotions to customers' preferences, previous purchases, and even their geographic location.

In addition, CRM frameworks enable advertisers with prescient examination abilities. By investigating authentic information inside the CRM, advertisers can recognize examples and patterns, empowering them to make information driven forecasts about client conduct. When it comes to anticipating customer requirements, optimizing marketing strategies, and even forecasting trends in sales, this foresight is invaluable.

Mechanization is another key component that CRM frameworks offer of real value in information driven showcasing. Through the incorporation of robotization apparatuses, advertisers can smooth out different cycles, from lead supporting to email crusades. Not only does automation improve productivity, but it also ensures that marketing efforts are timely and pertinent. For instance, an online business stage coordinated with CRM could mechanize customized email crusades set off by unambiguous client ways of behaving, like deserted trucks or ongoing buys.

In the time of information protection concerns, CRM frameworks likewise assume a vital part in guaranteeing consistency. These frameworks give a solid structure with overseeing and safeguarding client information, complying to guidelines like GDPR and CCPA. By executing strong safety efforts and consent controls, CRM frameworks empower organizations to fabricate entrust with their clients, guaranteeing them that their information is taken care of capably.

Besides, CRM frameworks work with constant correspondence and cooperation inside associations. Showcasing, deals, and client support groups can get to a similar unified data set, guaranteeing a consistent progression of data. Because of this synergy, teams are able to respond promptly to customer inquiries, resolve issues, and coordinate efforts to maximize customer satisfaction, all of which enhance the customer experience.

All in all, the joining of CRM frameworks in information driven showcasing addresses a change in outlook in how organizations associate with their clients. These frameworks engage advertisers with a 360-degree perspective on their client base, empowering them to make exceptionally focused on and customized crusades. From division and robotization to prescient examination and consistency, CRM frameworks act as the key part that changes crude client information into noteworthy experiences, cultivating more grounded and more significant connections among organizations and their customers. CRM systems will undoubtedly continue to be at the forefront of marketing innovation and efficiency as the landscape of marketing continues to change.

Chapter 3
Leveraging Data for Customer Insights

In today's data-driven marketing landscape, it is essential to use data to gain insight into customers. As organizations explore through a tremendous ocean of data, extricating significant bits of knowledge from information has turned into an essential objective. This cycle improves independent direction as well as empowers advertisers to fit their methodologies to meet the steadily developing necessities of their clients.

At the center of information driven advertising is the capacity to gather, break down, and decipher huge measures of information produced by client connections. The most vital phase in this excursion includes the orderly assortment of significant data of interest. This could incorporate client socioeconomics, buy history, online way of behaving, and virtual entertainment commitment. The objective is to make an extensive dataset that gives a 360-degree perspective on every client.

When the information is gathered, the subsequent stage is to successfully dissect it. Progressed examination devices and calculations assume a vital part in revealing examples, patterns, and relationships inside the information. For example, organizations can utilize prescient examination to figure client conduct, recognizing potential beat gambles or anticipating future buying designs. This considers proactive direction as well as helps in the advancement of designated showcasing efforts.

Another important aspect of using customer data to gain insights is segmentation. By separating the client base into particular portions in light of normal attributes or ways of behaving, advertisers can tailor their methodologies for each gathering. A retail company might, for instance, create segments based on how people shop, such as those who buy frequently, on occasion, or prefer to shop online. Each fragment can then be designated with explicit advancements or customized content.

Personalization is a foundation of successful information driven showcasing. Businesses are able to create highly personalized experiences with in-depth understanding of individual customer preferences. This goes past tending to clients by their most memorable name in email correspondences; it includes fitting item proposals, content, and advancements to match explicit interests and needs. Customized encounters upgrade consumer loyalty as well as encourage brand steadfastness.

The reconciliation of man-made brainpower (computer based intelligence) and AI (ML) innovations further enhances the force of information driven promotion. These advancements can robotize the examination of tremendous datasets progressively, empowering advertisers to answer quickly to changing business sector elements. Simulated intelligence driven chatbots, for example, can draw in with clients continuously, proposing customized suggestions in light of their past corporations and inclinations.

Besides, the utilization of information for client experiences stretches out past showcasing efforts. It assumes a significant part in forming the general client venture. Understanding the client's involvement with each touchpoint permits organizations to advance and refine their cycles. For example, by breaking down client criticism and collaboration information, organizations can distinguish trouble spots in their administration conveyance and execute upgrades to improve the general client experience.

Measurement and attribution of marketing efforts are also part of data-driven marketing. Attribution demonstrating permits organizations to comprehend which channels and touchpoints contribute most to changes. This understanding is significant in enhancing advertising spending plans and distributing assets to the best channels. It assists organizations with creating some distance from a one-size-fits-all way to deal with a more designated and proficient promoting technique.

Moral contemplations are fundamental in utilizing client information for advertising bits of knowledge. Transparency and safe data handling practices must be prioritized by businesses in light of increased scrutiny of data privacy. In order to build and maintain trust, it is essential to obtain explicit consent for the collection of data, ensure data security, and give customers control over their information.

All in all, utilizing information for client bits of knowledge isn't simply a pattern; It represents a significant shift in how businesses approach marketing. The capacity to tackle the force of information engages advertisers to figure out their clients at a granular level, empowering them to make customized and effective encounters. In our current reality where client assumptions are continually developing, information driven showcasing isn't simply a benefit - it's a need for remaining serious and important in the commercial center.

Customer Segmentation and Personalization Strategies

Client division and personalization are essential parts of information driven showcasing techniques, enabling organizations to interface with their crowd in a more designated and viable way. In the present unique commercial center, where buyers are immersed with data, understanding and utilizing information for division and personalization is urgent for remaining cutthroat.

Segmentation of Customers: Revealing Designated Crowds

Client division includes partitioning a wide objective market into more modest, more reasonable gatherings in view of shared qualities. In an information driven approach, this is accomplished by breaking down different data of interest, like socioeconomics, conduct, and inclinations. The goal is to find segments that have a lot in common so that marketers can tailor their strategies to meet specific expectations and needs.

Segment Division: This exemplary methodology sorts shoppers in light old enough, orientation, pay, and other segment factors. For example, a dress retailer could make various lobbies for youthful grown-ups and moderately aged experts.

Social Division: It's important to know how customers use a product or service. Businesses are able to classify customers based on their behavior by analyzing their purchase history, website engagement, and response to marketing campaigns, allowing them to tailor strategies to their preferences.

Psychographic Division: This dives into the way of life, values, and interests of customers. For example, a movement organization could make various advancements for experienced searchers and extravagance explorers.

Geographic Division: Marketing messages can be tailored by taking into account factors specific to a location. Relevance in a variety of markets is ensured by taking climate, cultural differences, and regional preferences into consideration.

Technographic Division: In the computerized age, understanding the innovation inclinations of clients is fundamental. This can incorporate the gadgets they use, favored stages, and online ways of behaving.

Personalization: Creating Exceptional Encounters

Personalization goes past division, zeroing in on fitting individual encounters for clients. It includes utilizing information to see every client's interesting inclinations and conveying significant substance, item proposals, or advancements. This makes a seriously captivating and fulfilling connection, encouraging client dedication.

Redone Content: Examining information on client inclinations permits organizations to make content that reverberates. Whether it's email crusades, blog entries, or item proposals, customized content upgrades commitment.

Item Proposals: Internet business stages succeed in utilizing personalization to recommend items in view of past buys, perusing history, and comparative clients' inclinations. This lifts deals as well as upgrades the client's shopping experience.

Personalized Communication: Customer engagement can be significantly impacted by personalized email, push notification, or social media message communication. A feeling of connection is created when customers are addressed by name and relevant information is provided.

Website Personalization in a Dynamic Way: Sites can be progressively redone in view of client conduct. From customized points of arrival to suggested items, this approach improves the general client experience.

Versatile Evaluating Models: A few businesses use personalization in estimating techniques, offering limits or advancements in view of individual way of behaving or steadfastness. Customers are drawn in, and revenue is maximized as a result.

Information Driven Promoting: The Power of Segmentation and Personalization The efficient use of data is fundamental to both customer segmentation and personalization. Progressed investigation instruments and AI calculations empower organizations to handle tremendous measures of information to infer significant experiences. This is the way information driven promoting energizes these methodologies:

Prescient Investigation: Businesses are able to predict the behavior of future customers by analyzing historical data. This empowers proactive division and personalization, expecting client needs and inclinations.

Continuous Information Handling: With the approach of continuous examination, organizations can answer client conduct in a flash. This is especially important in personalization, where convenient proposals or offers can essentially affect navigation.

Mapping the Customer's Journey: Information permits organizations to plan the whole client venture. The creation of streamlined, individualized experiences across various channels is made easier with an understanding of touchpoints and interactions.

A/B Testing and Improvement: Information driven promoting includes consistent testing and streamlining. Advertisers can try different things with various division approaches and personalization methodologies, refining their strategies in light of ongoing information.

Challenges and Moral Contemplations

While the advantages of client division and personalization are obvious, organizations should explore difficulties and moral contemplations related with information driven showcasing.

Security Concerns: Gathering and using client information raises security concerns. Finding some kind of harmony among personalization and regarding client protection is pivotal to building trust.

Information Precision: Depending on wrong or obsolete information can prompt off track division and personalization. Consistently refreshing and approving information is fundamental for powerful procedures.

Algorithmic Inclination: AI calculations might propagate predispositions present in authentic information. Organizations should effectively address and relieve inclinations to guarantee fair and even handed personalization.

Over-Dependence on Information: While information is strong, advertisers shouldn't exclusively depend on it. Offsetting information driven bits of knowledge with imagination and instinct is indispensable for an all encompassing showcasing technique.

The Eventual fate of Client Driven Advertising

As innovation progresses, client division and personalization will keep on advancing. Organizations that embrace information driven advertising and explore moral contemplations will be better situated to make significant associations with their crowd. Finding some kind of harmony among personalization and security, utilizing progressed examination, and remaining dexterous in adjusting systems will characterize the outcome of client driven advertising in the years to come.

Predictive Analytics in Customer Behavior

Prescient examination assumes a critical part in the domain of information driven promoting, especially with regards to understanding and impacting client conduct. As organizations explore the mind boggling scene of purchaser inclinations, utilizing prescient examination has turned into an essential goal. Data can be used to predict future trends, identify patterns, and improve marketing strategies to increase customer engagement with this powerful tool.

At its center, prescient investigation includes the utilization of factual calculations and AI procedures to dissect authentic information and make forecasts about future results. With regards to client conduct in information driven showcasing, this makes an interpretation of the capacity to guess how clients will answer different advertising drives. By mining immense datasets, organizations can reveal significant experiences that guide direction and improve the general viability of their advertising endeavors.

The capacity to create highly targeted and personalized marketing campaigns is one of the main benefits of predictive analytics in customer behavior. Through the examination of past client collaborations, buying history, and online way of behaving, organizations can create a nuanced comprehension of individual inclinations. Furnished with this data, advertisers can tailor their informing and advancements to reverberate with every client on an individual level, improving the probability of transformation.

Besides, prescient examination empowers organizations to distinguish potential high-esteem clients and spotlight their endeavors on developing these connections. Companies can devise strategies for attracting and retaining similar customers by analyzing patterns associated with devoted and profitable customers. This improves consumer loyalty as well as contributes essentially to the main concern.

In the time of enormous information, the sheer volume of data can overpower. Marketers can use predictive analytics as a compass to navigate the sea of data and find relevant trends and insights. Whether it's investigating virtual entertainment commitment, email open rates, or site associations, prescient examination distills these pieces of information into noteworthy insight. This permits advertisers to come to informed conclusions about which channels and messages are probably going to resound with their interest group.

Also, prescient examination enables advertisers to expect shifts in client conduct before they happen. By distinguishing early pointers and unobtrusive changes in designs, organizations can proactively change their methodologies to remain on the ball. In a dynamic market where customer preferences can change quickly, this forward-looking strategy is invaluable.

Client division is another region where prescient examination succeeds. Instead of depending on wide segment classifications, organizations can make more nuanced sections in view of prescient models. This guarantees that promoting endeavors are coordinated towards bunches with comparative ways of behaving and inclinations, bringing about additional designated and compelling efforts.

Customer retention is just as important as new customer acquisition in the data-driven marketing competitive landscape. Prescient examination supports anticipating client stir by distinguishing factors that add to steady loss. By understanding the signs that go before client surrender, organizations can carry out maintenance systems to moderate these dangers. This could include customized offers, designated correspondence, or different drives pointed toward supporting client reliability.

The coordination of prescient examination with showcasing robotization stages has additionally raised its effect. Mechanized frameworks can use prescient models to convey continuous, customized content to clients in light of their way of behaving and inclinations. This improves the client experience as well as smoothes out showcasing work processes, permitting groups to zero in on essential decision-production as opposed to manual execution.

Notwithstanding, it's fundamental to perceive that the adequacy of prescient examination in client conduct is dependent upon information quality and moral contemplations. Exact expectations depend on complete, precise, and fair-minded information. In this way, organizations should focus on information trustworthiness and address any predispositions present in their datasets to guarantee the dependability of prescient models.

All in all, prescient examination in client conduct is a unique advantage in information driven promoting. It enables businesses to adopt proactive, data-driven strategies as opposed to reactive ones. By grasping client inclinations, anticipating future patterns, and improving promoting endeavors, organizations can remain in front of the opposition and cultivate enduring associations with their ideal interest group. As innovation keeps on propelling, the job of prescient examination in molding the eventual fate of promoting is simply set to develop, making it an irreplaceable apparatus for organizations endeavoring to remain at the very front of their enterprises.

Chapter 4 Campaign Optimization

through Data and A/B Testing

Crusade improvement through information and A/B testing is a critical technique in present day showcasing, engaging organizations to refine their methodology, upgrade execution, and expand profit from venture. In the unique scene of computerized promotion, where patterns develop quickly, utilizing information driven experiences and A/B testing procedures is vital for remaining on top of things.

Campaign Optimization and Data Understanding:

Information fills in as the foundation of compelling effort advancement. Marketers are able to make well-informed decisions, recognize patterns, and comprehend user behavior thanks to the collection and analysis of pertinent data. This interaction includes utilizing key execution pointers (KPIs, for example, navigate rates, change rates, and commitment measurements.

By diving into information examination, advertisers can acquire significant bits of knowledge into the qualities and shortcomings of their missions. For example, understanding which channels drive the most changes or distinguishing segment sections that answer well to explicit informing engages advertisers to successfully tailor their missions more.

The Job of A/B Testing:

Split testing, also known as A/B testing, compares two or more different versions of a campaign element to see which one performs better. This iterative interaction permits advertisers to improve different parts of their missions, including promotion duplicate, visuals, embolden fastens, and in any event, points of arrival.

With regards to crusade improvement, A/B testing fills in as an incredible asset for refining procedures in light of genuine client corporations. For instance, testing different promotion titles can uncover which one resounds more with the interest group, prompting higher navigate rates.

Steps in Data and A/B Testing-Based Campaign Optimization:

Define KPIs and Objectives:

It is essential to clearly define objectives and key performance indicators prior to beginning a campaign. Having measurable metrics in place is essential, regardless of whether the objective is to boost brand awareness, increase conversions, or traffic to the website.

Information Assortment and Examination:

Execute vigorous information assortment systems to assemble data about client connections, inclinations, and transformation ways. Analyze this data with the help of analytics tools to spot patterns and areas that need improvement.

Division and Focusing on:

Influence information to portion your crowd in light of socio economics, conduct, or other significant variables. Tailor your missions to explicit fragments, guaranteeing a more customized and significant methodology.

A/B Testing Arrangement:

Plan A/B testing tries different things with an unmistakable theory and clear cut factors. This could include testing different promotion creatives, titles, point of arrival formats, or even the planning of your missions.

Run Analyses:

Execute your A/B tests by running the two forms at the same time. Guarantee that the tests are directed under comparative circumstances to get precise outcomes.

Screen and Dissect Results:

Routinely screen the exhibition of every variety during the A/B testing period. Break down the outcomes to recognize genuinely tremendous contrasts in measurements, for example, navigate rates, transformation rates, and commitment.

Iterative Enhancement:

In light of the A/B testing results, emphasize and refine your missions. Execute changes to the failing to meet expectations components and keep testing to track down the best procedures.

Scale Fruitful Varieties:

When decisive outcomes are acquired, scale the fruitful varieties across your missions. This guarantees that the improvements made through A/B testing add to the general progress of your showcasing endeavors.

Advantages of Mission Streamlining through Information and A/B Testing:

Increased Rates of Conversion:

Marketers can find the most compelling elements that resonate with their target audience through A/B testing, resulting in higher conversion rates.

Cost Effectiveness:

Marketers can better allocate resources, reduce costs, and maximize return on investment by optimizing campaigns based on data-driven insights.

Further developed Client Experience:

Understanding client conduct through information examination empowers the production of missions that line up with crowd inclinations, bringing about a more certain and drawing in client experience.

Adaptation to Changes in the Market:

A/B testing makes it easier to quickly adapt to changes in the market in the fast-paced digital environment. Advertisers can rapidly recognize and answer shifts in client conduct or industry patterns.

Improved Showcasing return for capital invested:

Crusade streamlining through information and A/B testing straightforwardly adds to further developed profit from venture by guaranteeing that assets are centered around systems demonstrated to be compelling.

For marketers aiming to remain competitive and achieve sustained success, campaign optimization through data and A/B testing is a strategic necessity. By utilizing the force of information examination and efficiently testing varieties, organizations can refine their showcasing systems, connect with their crowd all the more successfully, and at last drive predominant outcomes in an always advancing computerized scene.

Conversion Rate Optimization

Change Rate Enhancement (CRO) is a critical part of information driven showcasing techniques, zeroing in on improving the productivity of a site or computerized stage to change over guests into clients. In the powerful scene of web based showcasing, organizations endeavor to boost their profit from venture (return on initial capital investment), making CRO an imperative device for accomplishing this goal.

At its center, CRO depends on information investigation to distinguish and carry out enhancements that lead to higher change rates. Information driven promoting influences different examination devices to assemble experiences into client conduct, inclinations, and communications with a site. By deciphering this information, advertisers can recognize problem areas in the client venture, comprehend what works, and improve the transformation pipe appropriately.

One of the principal parts of CRO is A/B testing. Variations of a website or marketing component are created and distributed to various user groups using this strategy. Marketers can then determine which version has the highest conversion rates by measuring its performance. Businesses can improve their strategy without relying on presumptions by using A/B testing.

A clear set of goals is the first step in a data-driven CRO strategy. Having specific goals enables marketers to accurately measure success, whether it be increasing product purchases, signing up for newsletters, or any other desired action. This objective situated approach guarantees that all resulting examination and enhancement endeavors are lined up with the general business targets.

Client experience (UX) assumes an essential part in CRO. Information driven advertisers dig into client venture examination to recognize potential grating focuses that might dissuade clients from changing over. By streamlining the client experience through better route, responsive plan, and natural points of interaction, organizations can improve the general transformation rate.

Division is one more key component in information driven CRO. Investigating information in light of client sections permits advertisers to fit their procedures to various crowd gatherings. By understanding the exceptional requirements and ways of behaving of different fragments, advertisers can customize content, offers, and suggestions to take action, improving the probability of changes.

Information driven advertisers likewise use heatmaps and meeting accounts to acquire further bits of knowledge into client conduct. Heatmaps outwardly address the region of a page that draws in the most consideration or commitment. Meeting accounts give a granular perspective on individual client communications, assisting advertisers with understanding how clients explore through the site. With the help of these tools, you can find patterns and areas that need to be improved for better conversion rates.

Executing a strong investigation foundation is basic for effective CRO. By following and estimating key execution pointers (KPIs, for example, skip rate, time on page, and navigate rates, advertisers can constantly assess the effect of advancement endeavors. Constant information enables advertisers to pursue informed choices and quickly adjust methodologies in view of client reactions.

In the domain of web based business, truck relinquishment is a typical test. This problem is addressed by data-driven CRO strategies by identifying the causes of abandoned carts and implementing specific solutions. This could include upgrading the checkout cycle, giving straightforward valuing data, or offering customized motivating forces to empower fruition of the buy.

Personalization is a foundation of viable CRO. Information driven advertising permits organizations to use client information to make customized encounters. From customized item suggestions to custom-made email crusades, customization improves commitment and cultivates a feeling of association with the brand, eventually prompting higher change rates.

Data-driven CRO is built for continuous iteration. User preferences shift, the digital landscape changes, and new technologies emerge. By remaining nimble and receptive to information bits of knowledge, advertisers can repeat on their systems, adjusting to shifts on the lookout and keeping an upper hand.

All in all, Change Rate Enhancement in information driven showcasing is a multi-layered approach that depends on examination, testing, and consistent refinement. By utilizing information to comprehend client conduct, streamlining client encounters, and customizing communications, organizations can deliberately further develop their change rates. In a consistently developing computerized scene, a pledge to information driven CRO is fundamental for boosting the viability of showcasing endeavors and accomplishing maintainable business development.

Tracking and Analyzing Marketing Metrics

Following and examining promoting measurements is principal in the contemporary business scene, where information driven dynamic rules. In the powerful domain of advertising, understanding the exhibition of different techniques and channels is significant for upgrading efforts, improving return on initial capital investment, and remaining in front of the opposition.

At the core of compelling advertising estimation lies the recognizable proof of key execution markers (KPIs). These are quantifiable measurements that give experiences into the achievement or weaknesses of a showcasing effort. Normal advertising KPIs incorporate change rates, client securing cost (CAC), client lifetime esteem (CLV), and profit from speculation (return on initial capital investment).

Transformation rates, a crucial KPI, enlighten the viability of transforming possibilities into clients. By following the level of guests who make an ideal move, for example, making a buy or pursuing a pamphlet, advertisers gain significant experiences into the productivity of their pipe. Examining change rates recognizes bottlenecks and regions for development in the client venture.

Similarly basic is the assessment of client procurement cost, which addresses the costs caused to gain another client. By contrasting CAC and the income created from these clients, organizations can survey the expense adequacy of their securing methodologies. This measurement is fundamental in guaranteeing that advertising drives contribute decidedly to the reality.

Supplementing CAC, client lifetime esteem gives a comprehensive point of view on client connections. By assessing the complete income a client is supposed to create over their whole commitment with the brand, advertisers can settle on informed conclusions about asset portion and client maintenance endeavors. A high CLV shows solid client dedication and a sound long haul business viewpoint.

Profit from venture epitomizes the general exhibition of showcasing efforts by estimating the proportion of net benefit to the expenses caused. A Certain return for capital invested assists advertisers with measuring the productivity of their drives and allot assets to the most rewarding channels. A positive return for capital invested is a definitive objective, guaranteeing that showcasing endeavors contribute seriously to the organization's monetary achievement.

In the computerized age, online examination devices assume a vital part in following and deciphering these measurements. Stages like Google Investigation, HubSpot, and Adobe Examination offer far reaching information on site traffic, client conduct, and mission execution. Utilizing these devices enables advertisers to settle on information driven choices, refine methodologies continuously, and upgrade their advanced presence.

Virtual entertainment measurements structure one more basic part of promoting investigation. Commitment measurements on stages like Facebook, Instagram, and Twitter give significant experiences into crowd connection. A nuanced understanding of the performance of a piece of content can be obtained from its click-through rates, likes, shares, comments, and other metrics. This enables marketers to tailor their messages so that they resonate with their target audience.

Email showcasing measurements, like open rates, navigate rates, and transformation rates, are instrumental in assessing the viability of email crusades. Breaking down these measurements empowers advertisers to refine their email procedures, section their crowd, and convey customized content that reverberates with beneficiaries.

As advertising channels keep on broadening, the requirement for cross-channel examination turns out to be more articulated. A unified view of the customer journey is provided by unified marketing analytics platforms that aggregate data from various channels. This incorporated methodology permits advertisers to recognize examples, connections, and amazing open doors for streamlining across different touchpoints.

Notwithstanding quantitative measurements, subjective bits of knowledge from client input and reviews give a more profound comprehension of the client experience. Subjective information supplements quantitative measurements by offering setting and uncovering subtleties that may not be obvious through numbers alone. Client opinions, inclinations, and trouble spots gathered from subjective exploration illuminate advertising systems and upgrade by and large consumer loyalty.

Constant observing and examination of promoting measurements are fundamental for remaining deft in a quickly developing business scene. Standard audits empower advertisers to adjust to changing shopper conduct, arising patterns, and industry elements. A proactive way to deal with investigation positions organizations to jump all over chances, moderate dangers, and keep an upper hand.

All in all, following and examining promoting measurements is a foundation of effective and versatile showcasing procedures. By utilizing quantitative and subjective experiences, organizations can tweak their missions, streamline asset assignment, and at last drive manageable development. In today's data-driven world, successful marketers stand out from the competition in their quest for market relevance and consumer engagement by being able to extract actionable insights from marketing metrics.

Chapter 5 Case Studies and Successful stories on Data-Driven Marketing Campaigns

Businesses are able to tailor their strategies in order to achieve the best results thanks to data-driven marketing campaigns, which make use of insights and analytics to support decision-making. We should investigate a couple of convincing contextual investigations and examples of overcoming adversity that embody the viability of information driven promoting.

Netflix's Personalization Methodology:

Netflix, a trailblazer in information driven showcasing, uses watcher information to customize content suggestions. By breaking down client conduct, seeing history, and inclinations, Netflix's calculation proposes motion pictures and Network programs custom fitted to individual preferences. This approach altogether improves client commitment and maintenance, exhibiting the force of utilizing client information for customized promotion.

Amazon's Dynamic Item Suggestions:

Amazon has excelled at information driven advertising through its dynamic item suggestion motor. Amazon predicts what products customers might be interested in by examining customer browsing history, purchase patterns, and demographic data. This customized approach adds to higher transformation rates and expanded consumer loyalty, showing the effect of information driven bits of knowledge on web based business.

Spotify's Recommended Playlist:

Spotify utilizes information examination to organize customized playlists for its clients. By examining listening propensities, classes, and client produced playlists, Spotify's calculations make redid playlists that resound with individual inclinations. This improves the client experience as well as fills in as an incredible asset for advancing new music and craftsmen, displaying the effect of information driven promotion in the music streaming industry.

Target's Pregnancy Expectation Model:

Target's information driven advertising example of overcoming adversity spins around its capacity to foresee clients' life altering situations, especially pregnancy. Target's algorithm could identify subtle shifts in shopping behavior that indicates a customer might be expecting by analyzing purchasing patterns. Target then, at that point, sent customized offers and advancements, displaying the viability of information driven experiences in expecting client needs.

Airbnb's Dynamic Valuing Methodology:

Airbnb uses information investigation to execute a unique valuing model that changes rental rates in view of different factors like interest, irregularity, and nearby occasions. This data-driven strategy makes sure that hosts make the most money possible while keeping their prices low for guests. Airbnb's outcome in the excursion rental market features the significance of utilizing information for evaluating advancement in the sharing economy.

HubSpot's Inbound Showcasing Achievement:

HubSpot, a main promoting computerization stage, underlines the force of inbound showcasing through satisfied creation and designated crusades. By dissecting client cooperations with content, web-based entertainment commitment, and lead conduct, HubSpot tailors its showcasing endeavors to draw in, connect with, and enchant clients. This approach has prompted critical client obtaining and maintenance, displaying the effect of information driven techniques in inbound advertising.

The Personalized Share a Coke Campaign of Coca-Cola:

The "Share a Coke" campaign by Coca-Cola is an excellent illustration of using data to personalize large-scale marketing. The mission included printing famous names on Coke containers, and information examination was significant in figuring out which names to incorporate. By utilizing information on well known names and socioeconomics, Coca-Cola made a customized and shareable experience, driving buyer commitment and supporting deals.

American Express' Independent company Experiences:

American Express uses information driven experiences to offer some benefit to its private company clients. Through the Private venture Experiences stage, Amex investigates exchange information to propose customized suggestions and bits of knowledge to organizations. This engages private companies to pursue informed choices and advance their tasks, showing the effect of information driven advertising in supporting business development.

Taking everything into account, these contextual analyses highlight the extraordinary force of information driven advertising efforts across different ventures. Whether it's personalization in diversion, dynamic valuing in online business, prescient displaying in retail, or bits of knowledge driven systems in promoting stages, the ongoing idea is the viable utilization of information examination to illuminate navigation and improve client encounters. As organizations keep on outfitting the capability of information driven promoting, these examples of overcoming adversity act as motivation for others hoping to explore the developing scene of current showcasing.

Lessons Learned from Marketing Analytics Failures

Showcasing investigation disappointments can be significant educators, offering experiences that make ready for future achievement. In the powerful scene of computerized showcasing, organizations frequently convey refined examination devices to acquire an upper hand. However, these instruments are not error-free, and erroneous use can result in costly errors. How about we investigate a few key examples gained from promoting examination disappointments.

One normal entanglement is the overreliance on vanity measurements. Numerous advertisers fall into the snare of underlining measurements that look great on paper yet don't be guaranteed to relate with business achievement. Although metrics like website traffic, social media likes, or email open rates may appear promising, they rarely result in significant outcomes. The example here is to zero in on measurements straightforwardly attached to business goals, for example, transformation rates, client obtaining expenses, and lifetime esteem.

One more basic illustration includes the significance of information exactness. Erroneous or inadequate information can slant investigation results, prompting misinformed choices. Organizations ought to focus on information quality affirmation processes and routinely review their information sources. Moreover, laying out clear information administration strategies keeps up with consistency and unwavering quality in examination, guaranteeing that bits of knowledge are based on a strong groundwork.

Inability to adjust showcasing investigation within general business objectives is a typical slip up. Siloed examination endeavors can bring about separated techniques that neglect to add to the association's more extensive goals. The illustration is to incorporate advertising examination into the general business methodology, guaranteeing that bits of knowledge illuminate decision-production at each level. A holistic approach that maximizes the financial impact of marketing efforts is fostered by this alignment.

Lacking comprehension of the interest group is a predominant issue in showcasing examination disappointments. Essentially gathering information isn't sufficient; interpreting that information with regards to client conduct and preferences is significant. This illustration accentuates the requirement for powerful client division and persona advancement. Fitting showcasing techniques to explicit crowd fragments in light of thorough information examination prompts more customized and compelling efforts.

The inability to adjust to changing business sector elements is an exorbitant oversight. In the speedy advanced scene, purchaser conduct, innovation, and market patterns develop quickly. Static showcasing investigation models become outdated rapidly. The illustration here is to embrace readiness and routinely rethink and update examination procedures to remain on the ball. Nonstop learning and variation are fundamental parts of fruitful showcasing examination.

Another error in data analysis is to ignore the human factor. While investigation apparatuses give significant bits of knowledge, they miss the mark on capacity to grasp the subtleties of human way of behaving and feelings. The analysis gains depth by incorporating qualitative insights from customer feedback, surveys, and interviews with quantitative data. This example underscores the significance of a decent methodology that considers both the quantitative and subjective parts of promoting investigation.

Security and protection concerns have become progressively basic in the time of information driven showcasing. Forgetting to focus on information security can prompt penetrations that compromise client trust as well as result in legitimate outcomes. The illustration here is to carry out rigorous safety efforts, follow information assurance guidelines, and discuss straightforwardly with clients about information dealing with rehearses. Building trust is essential to long-term success in marketing analytics.

One illustration that frequently emerges from disappointments is the requirement for an obvious trial and error system. A/B testing and different types of trial and error are amazing assets for refining showcasing procedures. Nonetheless, without an organized methodology, these endeavors can yield uncertain or misdirecting results. Laying out clear speculations, choosing pertinent factors, and efficiently breaking down results add to the viability of trial and error in showcasing examination.

Inability to put resources into ability and preparation is a typical oversight. As innovation propels, promoting groups should persistently foster their insightful abilities to use the maximum capacity of accessible apparatuses. The example here is to focus on continuous preparation programs and draw in ability with a solid logical mentality. It is easier to navigate the complexities of marketing analytics and achieve meaningful outcomes with a team that is knowledgeable and skilled.

The lessons learned from failures in marketing analytics help shape strategies for the future. Each lesson contributes to a more effective and resilient approach to marketing analytics by addressing security concerns, implementing experimentation frameworks, investing in talent, prioritizing meaningful metrics, ensuring data accuracy, aligning with business goals, comprehending the audience, embracing agility, and considering the human element. As the computerized scene keeps on developing, associations that gain from their missteps and consistently refine their examination procedures will be better situated for progress.

Chapter 6 Ethical Considerations in Data-Driven Marketing

Information driven promoting is a useful asset that empowers organizations to grasp their interest group, customize messages, and enhance lobbies for improved results. Nonetheless, the broad utilization of information in showcasing raises significant moral contemplations that should be painstakingly addressed to guarantee purchaser security, straightforwardness, and fair practices.

One essential moral worry in information driven advertising rotates around buyer protection. There is a possibility of violating individuals' rights to privacy as businesses collect and analyze vast amounts of data to comprehend consumer behavior. It's critical for advertisers to embrace straightforward works on, advising buyers about the kinds regarding information gathered, how it will be utilized, and giving them the choice to quit.

Straightforwardness is the foundation of moral information driven advertising. Advertisers should be clear about their information assortment strategies, the reasons for which the information is used, and any potential outsider contribution. Giving shoppers exhaustive security arrangements and guaranteeing that they are effectively available is fundamental. This enables people to come to informed conclusions about sharing their own data and fabricates trust among shoppers and organizations.

Another moral thought includes the mindful utilization of buyer information. Advertisers should guarantee that the information they gather is utilized for genuine purposes and doesn't prompt biased rehearsals or the double-dealing of weak people. It is acceptable to use data to target specific demographics or personalize content, but it is unethical to go into discriminatory territory.

One potential gamble is algorithmic predisposition, where calculations may coincidentally propagate or try to enhance existing inclinations present in the information. Advertisers should effectively attempt to distinguish and redress such predispositions to guarantee fair and equivalent treatment, all things considered. Algorithm reviews and audits on a regular basis can help reduce these risks and encourage ethical data use.

Assent is a basic part of moral information driven promoting. Organizations should get express and informed assent from buyers prior to gathering and using their information. Assent ought to be a continuous cycle, and purchasers ought to have the choice to pull out their assent whenever. This approach regards individual independence and guarantees that buyers have command over their own data.

Security is another moral thought that can't be disregarded. Advertisers are answerable for protecting the information they gather from unapproved access, breaks, or abuse. Executing powerful safety efforts, including encryption and secure stockpiling rehearses, is basic to safeguard buyer data and keep up with trust.

Moreover, information minimization is a rule that moral advertisers ought to comply with. Gathering just the essential information for explicit purposes diminishes the gamble of likely abuse and keeps up with shopper trust. Pointless information assortment raises security worries as well as improves the probability of information breaks and digital dangers.

Ethical data-driven marketing also addresses the issue of data ownership. Customers ought to have clear freedoms with respect to their information, including the capacity to get to, right, or erase their data. Advertisers should regard these privileges and lay out components for people to practice command over their information.

Moral contemplations stretch out past the underlying assortment of information to its capacity and maintenance. Advertisers ought to lay out clear approaches on information maintenance periods, guaranteeing that information isn't held longer than needed for the expected purposes. Routinely cleansing obsolete or superfluous information limits the gamble of breaks and lines up with moral information the executives rehearses.

With regards to information driven advertising, the utilization of man-made reasoning (computer based intelligence) and AI presents extra moral difficulties. Advertisers should guarantee that simulated intelligence applications are straightforward, logical, and responsible. Understanding how calculations pursue choices is fundamental to forestall unseen side-effects and address any expected predispositions.

Moral promoting likewise includes mindful publicizing rehearsals. Advertisers ought to keep away from tricky strategies, deluding claims, or manipulative systems that could take advantage of customers. Accurate and transparent information fosters long-term customer relationships and builds trust and credibility.

Furthermore, advertisers need to consider the worldwide idea of information streams. With information frequently crossing worldwide lines, complying to various protection guidelines becomes essential. Moral advertisers ought to consent to material information insurance regulations and norms, perceiving and regarding the different lawful structures that oversee information protection around the world.

All in all, moral contemplations in information driven promoting are basic to building trust, guaranteeing shopper security, and cultivating dependable strategic approaches. Straightforwardness, assent, information minimization, security, and adherence to pertinent regulations are fundamental rules that guide moral decision-production in the steadily advancing scene of information driven showcasing. By focusing on moral contemplations, organizations can establish a positive and manageable promoting climate that benefits the two purchasers and the actual associations.

Privacy Concerns and Transparency and Consent

Security concerns, straightforwardness, and assent structure the foundation of moral contemplations in information driven advertising. As innovation propels, organizations progressively influence information to tailor their promoting systems, making customized encounters for shoppers. However, the ethical use of personal information is seriously questioned by this evolution.

The vast amounts of data that businesses collect, frequently without the explicit consent of customers, raise privacy concerns. This information includes all that from perusing propensities and web-based entertainment connections to area history and buy conduct. The sheer volume and granularity of this data raise alerts about likely abuse and unapproved access.

When addressing these issues, transparency takes on a crucial role.

Buyers reserve the option to understand what data is gathered, how it's utilized, and who approaches it. Organizations should be straightforward about what their information works on, giving clear and open protection arrangements. This straightforwardness enables people to arrive at informed conclusions about sharing their own data.

When it comes to ethical data use, consent is a crucial factor. It's tied in with acquiring authorization as well as guaranteeing that the assent is educated, explicit, and unreservedly given. Frequently, clients consent to agreements without completely understanding the ramifications, prompting a hole between what people accept they've assented to and the genuine utilization of their information.

Businesses must implement procedures that place an emphasis on privacy, openness, and informed consent in order to mitigate these issues. Implementing Privacy by Design, in which privacy concerns are incorporated into the design of goods and services from the outset, is one strategy. As a result of taking this proactive approach, privacy is not treated as an afterthought but rather as an essential component of the entire procedure.

Another way to address privacy concerns is to anonymize data. By eliminating by and by recognizable data, organizations can in any case determine significant experiences without imperiling individual protection. Notwithstanding, it's critical to perceive that total namelessness is trying to accomplish, and de-distinguished information can once in a while be re-distinguished through different means.

Straightforwardness in information driven advertising includes obviously imparting how information is gathered, handled, and utilized. This reaches out past lawful language in security arrangements to giving available clarifications to non-specialists. Organizations that embrace straightforwardness fabricate entrust with their crowd, cultivating a positive relationship that goes past simple exchanges.

It is crucial to inform customers about the benefits of data sharing. At the point when clients comprehend how their information adds to customized encounters, they might be more able to give assent. This instruction interaction ought to stress the equal idea of the connection among organizations and shoppers.

Finding some kind of harmony among personalization and protection requires cautious thought. While buyers value customized encounters, they are progressively careful about meddling showcasing strategies. Designated promotions that appear to realize a lot about people can feel obtrusive. Personalization must strike a balance between improving the user experience and protecting privacy.

Carrying out vigorous safety efforts is vital to shielding the information gathered. Information breaks undermine people's protection as well as dissolve trust in the organization's mindset. Normal reviews, encryption, and adherence to industry principles are fundamental parts of a complete information security system.

Administrative consistency is a vital part of tending to protection worries in information driven showcasing. Regulation like the Overall Information Security Guideline (GDPR) and the California Shopper Protection Act (CCPA) forces severe necessities on how organizations handle individual information. In addition to reducing legal risks, adhering to these regulations demonstrates a commitment to ethical data practices.

Moral information use reaches out to past lawful consistency. The broader societal consequences of a company's marketing strategies should be taken into account. This incorporates staying away from oppressive calculations and guaranteeing that information driven choices advance inclusivity as opposed to propagating inclinations.

Taking everything into account, security concerns, straightforwardness, and assent are primary components of moral information driven promoting. Organizations that focus on these standards construct trust, upgrade client connections, and add to a more mindful and supportable computerized environment. As innovation keeps on developing, organizations really must stay cautious in their obligation to moral information works on, perceiving that capable information use isn't simply a lawful prerequisite however an essential moral objective.

Chapter 7
Future Trends in Data-Driven Marketing

The scene of information driven promoting is ceaselessly developing, impelled by progressions in innovation, changes in purchaser conduct, and the powerful idea of the business climate. As we look forward, a few future patterns are ready to shape the direction of information driven promoting methodologies.

1.   Man-made   consciousness (artificial intelligence) Joining:

Artificial intelligence is turning into an essential piece of information driven promoting, offering complex apparatuses for information examination, personalization, and mechanization. Marketers can gain valuable insights and better predict consumer behavior thanks to machine learning algorithms' ability to analyze vast datasets. Artificial intelligence driven chatbots and menial helpers likewise upgrade client connections, giving customized encounters in light of information driven understanding.

2. Upgraded Client Personalization:

79

Information driven advertising is moving past fundamental personalization to hyper-personalization. Advanced analytics are being used by marketers to create highly targeted and individualized customer experiences. By dissecting client inclinations, ways of behaving, and authentic information, brands can tailor their informing, offers, and content, bringing about additional significant connections and expanded client dependability.

3. Security First Methodologies:

With expanding worries about information security, advertisers are moving towards protection first methodologies. Transparency in data collection and use is emphasized by stricter regulations like the GDPR and CCPA. Therefore, advertisers are zeroing in on building entrust with customers by embracing moral information works on, getting express assent, and guaranteeing secure information taking care of cycles.

4. Information Cooperation and Sharing:

Coordinated effort among associations to share non-delicate information is arising as a pattern. Businesses are able to gain more comprehensive insights without jeopardizing individual privacy through this cooperative strategy. Information sharing coalitions can be helpful for cross-industry examination, recognizing patterns, and upgrading the general adequacy of promoting methodologies.

5. Mix of Increased Reality (AR) and Augmented Reality (VR):

The use of augmented reality (AR) and virtual reality (VR) in marketing is gaining traction. These vivid advances empower brands to make drawing in and intelligent encounters for purchasers. From virtual item attempts to increased reality commercials, advertisers are investigating imaginative ways of utilizing these advancements for information driven crusades that catch consideration and drive commitment.

6. Voice Inquiry Streamlining:

Optimizing for voice search is becoming increasingly important as the number of voice-activated devices continues to rise. Advertisers are adjusting their techniques to line up with the conversational idea of voice search questions. Grasping client plans, fitting substance for spoken questions, and enhancing for highlighted bits are fundamental parts of a fruitful information driven voice search procedure.

7. Customer Retention Predictive Analytics:

Prescient examination is developing to assume a more huge part in client maintenance methodologies. By investigating authentic information and recognizing designs, prescient models can figure client stir, permitting advertisers to proactively address issues and carry out designated maintenance crusades. This proactive methodology can altogether influence client dedication and lifetime esteem.

8. Blockchain for Data Transparency and Security:

Blockchain innovation is acquiring consideration for upgrading information security and straightforwardness in marketing potential. By making decentralized and carefully designed records, blockchain can address concerns connected with information uprightness and legitimacy. This is especially applicable with regards to computerized publicizing, where false exercises and promotion misrepresentation are continuous difficulties.

9. Comprehensive Advertising and Variety Investigation:

In light of cultural moves and expanded consciousness of variety issues, advertisers are integrating variety examination into their procedures. Information driven bits of knowledge assist associations with grasping the assorted inclinations and ways of behaving of their interest groups. Comprehensive promoting plans to address a more extensive range of society, cultivating more grounded associations with different shopper portions.

10. Marketing that is driven by sustainability:

As ecological cognizance develops, supportability is turning into a critical concentration in promoting methodologies. Information driven approaches assist organizations with grasping the ecological effect of their activities and items. Advertisers can use this information to impart straightforwardly about supportability drives, measuring up to the assumptions of eco-cognizant customers.

Taking everything into account, the eventual fate of information driven showcasing is dynamic and formed by innovative headways, changing purchaser assumptions, and cultural patterns. Advertisers need to embrace these arising patterns to remain on the ball, guaranteeing that their methodologies stay important, viable, and morally sound in a consistently advancing scene.

Artificial Intelligence and Machine Learning

Man-made consciousness (artificial intelligence) and AI (ML) have arisen as extraordinary powers in the domain of information driven promoting, reforming how organizations dissect and use information to upgrade their advertising systems. In this time of digitalization, the overflow of information created by online exercises presents both a test and a chance for advertisers. Man-made intelligence and ML advancements assume a vital part in bridling this information to settle on informed choices, streamline crusades, and customize client encounters.

One of the essential commitments of computer based intelligence and ML in information driven advertising is their capacity to deal with huge measures of information rapidly and effectively. Customary advertising approaches frequently battled to adapt to the sheer volume and intricacy of information accessible. Artificial intelligence, furnished with cutting edge calculations, succeeds at taking care of large information, empowering advertisers to remove significant bits of knowledge and examples that would be almost difficult to physically perceive. This improved scientific ability frames the establishment for information driven dynamics in showcasing systems.

Prescient examination is a vital part of man-made intelligence and ML applications in information driven showcasing. By examining verifiable information and recognizing designs, these innovations can figure future patterns and buyer ways of behaving. This engages advertisers to expect market changes, client inclinations, and possible open doors, taking into consideration proactive and key direction. Prescient examination helps in streamlining promoting systems as well as helps in stock administration, valuing, and item improvement.

A key component of successful marketing is personalization, and AI-driven algorithms are crucial in providing customers with individualized experiences. Machine learning algorithms create targeted content and personalized recommendations by analyzing individual customer interactions, preferences, and behavior. This degree of personalization improves client commitment and fulfillment, encouraging more grounded brand dedication. AI enables marketers to create hyper-personalized experiences that resonate with their audience, from personalized email campaigns to targeted social media advertisements.

In marketing, AI-powered chatbots and virtual assistants are transforming customer interactions. These keen specialists give continuous reactions to client questions, present customized proposals, and guide clients through the buy venture. Via mechanizing client care and commitment, organizations can upgrade client experience, further develop reaction times, and smooth out correspondence processes. This not just opens up HR for additional essential errands yet additionally adds to building a positive brand picture through productive and customized client corporations.

AI has changed programmatic advertising in the digital advertising industry. Ad targeting and delivery are enhanced by automated buying and placement of advertisements based on real-time data and user behavior. Bidding strategies are adapted as a result of machine learning algorithms' analysis of large datasets to determine the audience segments that are most relevant. This works on the proficiency of promoting efforts as well as amplifies the profit from speculation by guaranteeing that advertisements are displayed to the ideal crowd with flawless timing.

Attribution demonstrating, a basic part of promoting examination, has likewise been fundamentally improved by simulated intelligence and ML. These advancements empower advertisers to precisely ascribe transformations and measure the effect of each touchpoint in the client venture. Businesses can better allocate resources, optimize their marketing mix, and enhance overall campaign performance by comprehending the contribution of various channels and touchpoints.

While simulated intelligence and ML offer various benefits in information driven promoting, moral contemplations and information security issues should be painstakingly tended to. The assortment and usage of client information raises worries about protection and security. Finding some kind of harmony between utilizing information for the purpose of advertising and regarding client protection is fundamental to keep up with trust and consistent with guidelines. All in all, Man-made reasoning and AI have introduced another period of information driven showcasing. The capacity to investigate tremendous datasets, foresee buyer conduct, customize encounters, and robotize processes has engaged advertisers to pursue more educated choices and make exceptionally focused on and viable missions. AI and machine learning (ML) will likely become more deeply integrated into marketing as technology advances, providing marketers with increasingly sophisticated tools to navigate the complex landscape of contemporary consumerism.

Emerging Technologies Impacting Marketing Analytics

Arising advances are reforming the field of promoting investigation, offering extraordinary open doors for organizations to acquire further experiences, upgrade focusing on procedures, and streamline by and large advertising execution. As we explore the always developing advanced scene, a few key innovations are molding the eventual fate of showcasing investigation.

1. Computerized reasoning and AI:

Marketing analytics has come to rely heavily on AI and ML, which make it possible for businesses to analyze vast datasets and derive useful insights. These innovations enable advertisers to foresee shopper conduct, customize content, and computerized dynamic cycles. Computer based intelligence calculations can dissect designs, recognize patterns, and make constant proposals, upgrading the proficiency and adequacy of advertising efforts.

2. Prescient Examination:

Prescient investigation uses verifiable information and high level calculations to conjecture future patterns and results. By utilizing AI models, advertisers can expect client inclinations, upgrade evaluating methodologies, and foresee market interest. This permits organizations to proactively change their promoting techniques, designate assets effectively, and remain in front of the opposition.

3. Increased Reality (AR) and Augmented Reality (VR):

AR and VR advances are changing the manner in which shoppers communicate with brands. Advertisers can make vivid encounters, permitting clients to attempt items prior to settling on a buy choice essentially. This upgrades commitment as well as gives significant information on purchaser inclinations and conduct. As AR and VR become more available, integrating these innovations into advertising examination will be vital for making noteworthy and effective missions.

4. Web of Things (IoT):

Data is gathered and exchanged by interconnected devices in the Internet of Things. In the domain of showcasing examination, IoT gadgets offer an abundance of data about customer conduct. From wearable gadgets that track wellness exercises to shrewd home gadgets that screen everyday schedules, this information can be utilized to make exceptionally focused on and customized advertising efforts. IoT empowers advertisers to comprehend the setting wherein customers draw in with items and administrations, prompting more viable correspondence methodologies.

5. Chatbots and Conversational simulated intelligence:

Chatbots controlled by conversational simulated intelligence are becoming fundamental devices in client associations. Customers can interact with these automated systems in real time, get answers to their questions, and get personalized recommendations. Past client assistance, chatbots contribute significant information for showcasing examination by catching client inclinations, figuring out goal, and recognizing likely regions for development in the client venture.

6. Technology of the Blockchain:

Blockchain isn't just inseparable from digital currencies; its decentralized nature can be bridled for promoting investigation. The transparency and accuracy of data are guaranteed by blockchain, lowering the likelihood of fraud and increasing consumer and business trust. Advertisers can utilize blockchain to follow the beginning of items, confirm the genuineness of client audits, and make more straightforward and responsible publicizing biological systems.

7. 5G Innovation:

The rollout of 5G organizations brings a quicker and more dependable web network. This has huge ramifications for advertising examination, especially in the domain of ongoing information handling. Advertisers can use 5G to gather and dissect information at uncommon velocities, empowering faster navigation and the conveyance of dynamic, customized content to buyers continuously.

8. Voice Search and Brilliant Speakers:

The rising predominance of voice-enacted gadgets and shrewd speakers has modified the manner in which clients look for data. Advertisers should adjust their systems to oblige voice search inquiries. Understanding the subtleties of voice search and streamlining content for this medium is fundamental for remaining applicable. Integrating voice information into examination models assists advertisers with acquiring bits of knowledge into client inclinations and adjusting their missions as needs be.

The effect of arising advances on promoting examination is groundbreaking, offering organizations the devices to comprehend, associate with, and take special care of their main interest group in exceptional ways. As computer based intelligence, AR, IoT, and different innovations keep on developing, advertisers should embrace these headways to remain cutthroat and convey more customized and viable missions. The eventual fate of advertising examination lies in the consistent joining of these advancements, empowering organizations to explore the intricacies of the computerized scene and open new degrees of accomplishment.

Chapter 8 Implementing a Data-Driven Marketing Strategy

Executing an information driven showcasing system is essential in the present computerized scene, where organizations approach huge measures of information that can illuminate and improve their promoting endeavors. This approach includes utilizing information bits of knowledge to go with informed choices, enhance crusades, and eventually drive improved results. An in-depth look at the most important steps and things to think about when putting a data-driven marketing strategy into action is provided here.

1. Grasping the Significance of Information:

Information is the groundwork of an information driven promoting technique. Customer preferences, demographics, and behavior are all included. By breaking down this data, organizations gain important experiences into their interest group, considering more customized and designated showcasing endeavors.

2. Defining Specific Objectives:

It is essential to establish precise marketing objectives prior to beginning data analysis. Whether it's rising image mindfulness, driving deals, or further developing client maintenance, having explicit objectives will direct your information driven endeavors and assist with estimating achievement.

3. Gathering Significant Information:

Distinguish the key information focuses that line up with your showcasing goals. Website analytics, social media metrics, customer feedback, and sales data are all examples of this. Guarantee that the information gathered is precise, exceptional, and agreeable with protection guidelines.

4. Using Stable Analytics Tools:

Putting resources into cutting edge investigation devices is fundamental for handling and deciphering huge datasets. Stages like Google Examination, Adobe Examination, or custom arrangements give top to bottom experiences into client conduct, crusade execution, and by and large promoting viability.

5. Data Source Integration:

Merge information from different sources to make an extensive perspective on your crowd. This might include coordinating CRM frameworks, web-based entertainment stages, and different information stores. A more comprehensive comprehension of customer interactions is made possible by a unified dataset.

6. Segmentation for Specified Ads:

Section your crowd in view of pertinent models like socioeconomics, conduct, or buy history. This division takes into account exceptionally designated and customized showcasing efforts, improving the probability of commitment and transformation.

7. Utilizing Analytical Prediction:

Execute prescient investigation to conjecture future patterns and client conduct. Businesses are able to anticipate changes in the market, adjust their strategies accordingly, and stay ahead of the competition thanks to this proactive approach.

8. Making decisions in real time:

Empower constant information examination to pursue informed choices on the fly. This is especially significant in powerful promoting conditions where speedy changes in accordance with missions can gain by arising open doors or address difficulties expeditiously.

9. Personalization Across Channels:

Tailor advertising messages and content in view of individual inclinations. Personalization increases conversion rates by strengthening customer relationships and enhancing the user experience as a whole.

10. A/B Testing for Improvement:

Lead A/B testing to try different things with various components of your missions, for example, promotion duplicate, visuals, or source of inspiration buttons. Dissect the outcomes to comprehend what reverberates best with your crowd and constantly enhance your promoting materials.

11. Carrying out AI:

Automate and improve decision-making processes by integrating machine learning algorithms. From foreseeing client inclinations to upgrading promotion arrangements, AI can altogether work on the productivity and viability of your showcasing technique.

12. Estimating and Emphasizing:

Consistently measure the presentation of your advertising efforts against predefined KPIs. Utilize these bits of knowledge to constantly emphasize and refine your procedure. An information driven approach includes a pattern of examination, streamlining, and refinement.

13. Guaranteeing Information Security and Consistence:

Focus on information security and consistence with guidelines like GDPR or CCPA. In addition to being required by law, protecting the privacy of your customers is essential for establishing trust with your audience.

14. Preparing Groups on Information Proficiency:

Enable your showcasing groups with the important abilities to actually decipher and use information. Information proficiency is a basic part of a fruitful information driven methodology, guaranteeing that bits of knowledge are perceived and applied properly.

15. Scaling Experiences Across the Association:

Data-driven marketing's advantages extend beyond the marketing department. Share bits of knowledge with different groups, for example, item advancement or client assistance, to illuminate more extensive business methodologies and improve the general client experience.

All in all, executing an information driven showcasing methodology is a diverse cycle that includes grasping the meaning of information, setting clear targets, gathering and coordinating significant information, and utilizing progressed examination devices. To remain agile in a dynamic market, it is an iterative procedure that necessitates ongoing measurement, analysis, and optimization. By embracing information driven direction, organizations can upgrade their showcasing endeavors, further develop client commitment, and at last drive maintainable development in the advanced period.

Steps for Successful Implementation and Overcoming Challenges

To accomplish fruitful execution and conquer difficulties in information driven promoting, organizations should follow a deliberate methodology. The interaction includes vital preparation, information assortment, examination, execution, and continuous advancement. Here are key stages to guarantee a smooth and successful change to information driven showcasing:

Characterize Clear Targets:

Begin by characterizing explicit objectives and targets for your information driven showcasing endeavors. Comprehend what you mean to accomplish, whether it's rising client commitment, driving deals, or further developing brand mindfulness.

Integration and data auditing:

Lead a far reaching review of your current information sources. Make sure that the relevant data points you find are in line with your marketing goals. Coordinate information from different sources, like client relationship, the executives (CRM) frameworks, virtual entertainment stages, and site investigation.

Put resources into Quality Information:

The outcome of information driven promotion depends on the nature of the information. Put resources into getting exact, dependable, and state-of-the-art information. Purify and approve information routinely to kill irregularities and mistakes.

Influence Progressed Examination:

Utilize progressed examination devices to separate significant experiences from the gathered information. Prescient investigation, AI, and man-made reasoning can assist with recognizing examples, inclinations, and patterns that conventional examination might ignore.

Make personalization a reality:

Utilize the bits of knowledge acquired from information examination to customize promoting messages and missions. Create content, offers, and recommendations that are based on the demographics, preferences, and behavior of your customers.

Personalization improves client commitment and increments change rates.

Integration across all channels:
Coordinate information across different promoting channels to make a bound together client experience. Reliable informing and consistent changes between channels add to a strong and powerful showcasing methodology.

Embrace Advertising Robotization:
Use marketing automation tools to make repetitive tasks like email campaigns, posting to social media, and nurturing leads easier. Automation not only helps you save time, but it also makes sure that your marketing efforts are consistent and accurate.

Conformity with Data Protection Laws:
Remain consistent with information security guidelines and protection regulations. Lay out hearty information administration strategies to defend client data. Straightforwardness about information use assembles entrust with clients and dodges lawful intricacies.

Representative Preparation:
Train your advertising group on information driven practices and devices. Make sure employees know how to interpret data insights and use them to make decisions. Consistent preparation keeps the group side by side of developing patterns in information driven advertising.

Screen Key Execution Pointers (KPIs):
Lay out and routinely screen KPIs applicable to your promoting goals. Measurements, for example, transformation rates, client securing

expenses, and profit from speculation give significant bits of knowledge into the viability of your information driven techniques.

Difficulties and Arrangements:

Information Security Concerns:

Challenge: Implementation can be hindered by security concerns, but protecting customer data is essential.

Solution: Encrypt sensitive data, implement robust cybersecurity measures, and regularly audit and update security protocols.

Issues with Integration:

Challenge: Coordinating information from unique sources can be complicated and may prompt irregularities.

Solution: Put resources into a unified information framework, and guarantee similarity between various stages to work with a smooth mix.

Change Resistance:

Challenge: Workers might oppose the shift towards an information driven approach.

Solution: Cultivate a culture of versatility, give preparing programs, and exhibit the advantages of information driven decision-production to beat obstruction.

Information Precision and Quality:

Challenge: Decisions and insights that are based on incorrect information can be made.

Solution: Consistently review and purge information, lay out information approval processes, and put resources into information quality instruments to keep up with precision.

Over Reliance on Innovation:

Challenge: Depending exclusively on innovation without human ability can prompt error of information.

Solution: Encourage marketing professionals, data scientists, and analysts to collaborate to strike a balance between technology and human insights.

Adjusting to Quick Innovative Changes:

Challenge: The promoting innovation scene advances rapidly, and remaining current can challenge.

Solution: Consistently evaluate and refresh your innovation stack, remain informed about industry drifts, and put resources into versatile arrangements.

All in all, fruitful execution of information driven promotion requires an essential methodology, a pledge to quality information, and the capacity to adjust to difficulties. By characterizing clear goals, utilizing progressed examination, and tending to key difficulties, organizations can open the maximum capacity of information driven showcasing and gain an upper hand in the powerful computerized scene.

CONCLUSION

Importance of Continuous

Adaptation in Data-Driven Marketing

The significance of using examination for informed dynamics in information driven showcasing couldn't possibly be more significant. The unique scene of the business world requests an essential methodology that goes past instinct and hunch. Examination furnishes advertisers with the instruments to interpret immense measures of information, extricate significant bits of knowledge, and settle on informed choices that drive effective missions.

One of the critical benefits of utilizing examination is the capacity to figure out buyer conduct. Through the investigation of information, advertisers can acquire significant experiences into client inclinations, buying examples, and commitment levels. This understanding empowers the formation of customized and designated showcasing efforts, which are undeniably bound to resound with the target group. In reality as we know it, where customers are immersed with data, the capacity to convey customized messages improves the probability of catching consideration and cultivating brand faithfulness.

Moreover, examinations enable advertisers to gauge the viability of their missions with accuracy. By following key execution pointers (KPIs, for example, transformation rates, navigate rates, and client obtaining costs, advertisers can survey the effect of their endeavors. This information driven approach considers fast changes and advancements, guaranteeing that showcasing techniques are spry and receptive to changing economic situations.

Persistent transformation is a foundation of effective information driven showcasing. The business scene is described by quick changes, and what works today may not be as successful tomorrow. Examination acts as a compass in this steadily moving landscape, directing advertisers to adjust their procedures in view of constant information. Whether it's changing promotion spend, refining ideal interest groups, or tweaking informing, the capacity to adjust rapidly is an upper hand in the quick moving universe of showcasing.

In addition, incorporating analytics into marketing strategies encourages a culture of accountability and open communication. With information driven experiences, promoting groups can exhibit the profit from speculation (return on initial capital investment) of their missions. This legitimizes promoting consumptions as well as works with information driven direction at all levels of the association. As examination becomes imbued in the hierarchical DNA, a culture of persistent improvement arises, driving development and effectiveness.

With regards to information driven promoting, the client venture becomes the overwhelming focus. Examination empowers advertisers to plan the whole client venture, from introductory attention to post-buy commitment. This all encompassing perspective takes into account the recognizable proof of touchpoints that fundamentally influence client independent direction. By streamlining these touchpoints, advertisers can make a consistent and charming client experience, improving brand insight and improving the probability of client maintenance.

Besides, the significance of investigation stretches out past individual missions to overall business procedure. Informed by information, associations can pursue vital choices that line up with market patterns and client assumptions. Whether it's venturing into new business sectors, presenting creative items, or refining estimating techniques, investigation gives the experiences important to sure and information driven decision-production at the essential level.

It is quite significant that the sheer volume of information accessible can overpower. Hence, the job of examination apparatuses and stages becomes significant in smoothing out the information investigation process. Mechanization and AI calculations assist advertisers with filtering through huge datasets, uncovering examples and patterns that may not be obvious through manual investigation. This recoveries time as well as improves the precision and profundity of experiences, empowering advertisers to pursue more educated choices.

All in all, the significance of utilizing examination for informed direction and the persistent variation in information driven advertising couldn't possibly be more significant. In a business climate portrayed by intricacy and steady change, examination give the compass expected to effectively explore the scene. From grasping purchaser conduct to estimating effort viability and adjusting procedures progressively, examination enables advertisers to remain on top of things. As associations embrace an information driven culture, the reconciliation of examination becomes a device as well as a central part of key direction, driving development and guaranteeing long haul progress in the unique universe of promoting.

DEAR READER

Your thoughts matter to us! If the book brought a smile or moment of respite, please Consider Sharing your experience through a review.
Your feedback is invaluable in making our book even more enjoyable for following.We hope this message finds you well and enjoying your literary adventures! We value the opinions of our readers, and we would love to hear your thoughts on **[DATA-DRIVEN MARKETING]**.
Thank you for being a part of our literary journey, and we look forward to reading your review!

WARM REGARDS

www.ingramcontent.com/pod-product-compliance
Lightning Source LLC
Chambersburg PA
CBHW071054290526
45795CB00004B/1483